THE CANADIAN BRASS

BOOK OF INTERMEDIATE TUBA SOLOS

Edited by **Charles Daellenbach** of **The Canadian Brass**

WITH COMPANION AUDIO

■

All Selections Performed by **Charles Daellenbach, tuba,**
and Patrick Hansen, Piano

■

Plus Piano Accompaniments Only

The instrument pictured on the cover is a CB50 Tuba from The Canadian Brass Collection,
a line of professional brass instruments marketed by The Canadian Brass.

Photo: Gordon Janowiak

PLAYBACK+
Speed • Pitch • Balance • Loop

To access audio visit:
www.halleonard.com/mylibrary

Enter Code
5636-3827-2479-5056

ISBN 978-0-7935-7256-4

HAL•LEONARD®

www.canadianbrass.com
www.halleonard.com

Contact us:
Hal Leonard
7777 West Bluemound Road
Milwaukee, WI 53213
Email: info@halleonard.com

In Europe, contact:
Hal Leonard Europe Limited
42 Wigmore Street
Marylebone, London, W1U 2RN
Email: info@halleonardeurope.com

In Australia, contact:
Hal Leonard Australia Pty. Ltd.
4 Lentara Court
Cheltenham, Victoria, 3192 Australia
Email: info@halleonard.com.au

CONTENTS

In progressive order of difficulty, from a generally intermediate to an advanced level.

To All Fellow Brass Players:

Those of us who teach and play brass instruments know what a struggle it can be to find interesting and beautiful solos for our instruments. We ourselves experienced the problem first hand in our younger days, and later have encountered the same shortage of solo material at various points in our lives when we have taught brass students. It's been an aim of ours to add to the solo repertory, and we are particularly pleased to add these collections to our library of Canadian Brass publications.

What makes a good brass solo? There is virtually no original literature for our instruments, beyond a handful of trumpet and horn concertos, before the twentieth century. So if, as brass players, we want to play Bach or Handel or Mozart or Brahms, then we must choose pieces written for other instruments to transcribe for our own. And how do we choose what to transcribe? In our opinion, vocal music offers the best solution for various reasons. The pieces are often short, which is best for a brass solo. The music is written originally to words, which makes each piece have a strong emotional content and point of view that can be very satisfying to play. Because in the broadest definition the voice could be defined as a wind instrument, the phrases and lines are naturally well suited for brass players. And further, there is simply far more solo music written for the voice than any other instrument in history. Composers seem to have been continually inspired by singers throughout the centuries, and we see no reason why we brass players shouldn't benefit from all that inspiration! After having said all of that, it will come as no surprise to state that most of the pieces we have chosen for these solo books are transcriptions of vocal pieces. Another priority in making the selections was to include mostly work by major composers from the history of music. Altogether too much of the educational solo music available almost exclusively presents work by minor or unknown composers.

The recordings we have made should be used only as a guide for you to use in studying a piece. We certainly didn't go into these recording sessions with the idea of trying to create any kind of "definitive performances" of this music. There is no such thing as a definitive performance anyway. Each musician, being a unique individual, will naturally always come up with a slightly different rendition of a piece of music. We often find that students are timid about revealing their own ideas and personalities when going beyond the notes on the page in making music. After you've practiced for weeks or months on a piece of music, and have mastered all the technical requirements, you certainly have earned the right to play it in the way you think it sounds best! It may not be the way your friend would play it, or the way The Canadian Brass would play it. But you will have made the music your own, and that's what counts.

Good luck and Happy Brass Playing!
The Canadian Brass

CHARLES DAELLENBACH, tuba player in The Canadian Brass, graduated from the Eastman School of Music at the age of twenty-five with a Ph.D. in music education. He then joined the music faculty at the University of Toronto, where he was head of the brass division. In 1970, collaborating with trombonist Eugene Watts, he helped found The Canadian Brass. The group became so successful so quickly that he soon had to devote his full time to performing and touring with the quintet. Charles' many interests have led him to become the businessman of The Canadian Brass, working closely with their managers, agents, lawyers, recording companies, and public representatives, as well as directing the group's ambitious publishing activities. Charles is a natural on any stage, and is the quintet's quick-witted elocutionist.

PATRICK HANSEN, pianist, has been musical coach and assistant conductor at Des Moines Metro Opera, and has served on the staff of Juilliard Opera Center as a coach and accompanist. He was assistant editor on the new G. Schirmer Opera Anthology, and has recorded several other albums for Hal Leonard. Patrick holds degress in piano from Simpson College and the University of Missouri at Kansas City.

ABOUT THE MUSIC...

Franz Schubert: To Music (An die Musik)

Schubert (pronounced SHU-bayrt) (1797-1828) was the first master of German song literature, or *lieder*. He composed over 600 songs for voice and piano during his lifetime, all of which are settings of German poets of his time (or occasionally German translations of other European poets). "An die Musik," composed in 1817, is an earnest ode to the art of music, and is one of Schubert's best known and most noble melodies.

Giacomo Puccini: Colline's Aria (from *La Bohème*)

La Bohème (translated "The Bohemian Life") just might be the most popular opera in the world. It's a story of struggling young writers, painters, and musicians in Paris of the 1830s. Colline is the philosopher among the characters. When Mimì, the writer Rodolpho's lover, becomes seriously ill with tuberculosis, Colline decides to sell his overcoat to the pawnbroker to help pay for her medical expenses. But before heading to the pawnshop, he sings a philosophical farewell to his old overcoat, and reflects on the many years that have passed since he first began to wear it. Colline is sung by a bass in the opera, and his ponderous tune suits the tuba very well. (Pronunciations: Puccini=pu-CHEE-nee, Colline=ko-LEE-nay, La Bohème=la bo-EHM)

Franz Schubert: Who Is Sylvia?

Occasionally Schubert, the master of German art song, chose to set to music a translation of a non-German writer, and "Who Is Sylvia?" is just such an instance. The text of this famous song is a German translation of a poem by Shakespeare. It's a ballad from his play *Two Gentleman of Verona*. The song is an ode to a woman named—you guessed it—Sylvia.

Gabriel Fauré: The Secret

Just as Schubert was a master of German art song, so was Fauré (pronounced four-AY) (1845-1924) a master of art songs in the French language. "The Secret" was composed about 1881 to a poem by Armand Silvestre. It's a gentle love song, and should be played with delicacy and great attention to phrasing.

George Frideric Handel: Where E'er You Walk

Handel (1685-1759) was one of the two musical giants of the Baroque (the other being J. S. Bach, of course). Handel spent most of his life in London, running an opera company, and writing 45 operas in 30 years. When he started losing money on opera in London, he switched to composing oratorio with equal fury, and easily kept his fame and fortune afloat. "Where E'er You Walk" is one of Handel's most famous tunes, written for the oratorio *Semele*, premiered at Covent Garden in 1744. The words are an ode to a beloved one: "Where E'er you walk, cool gales shall fan the glades. Trees where you sit shall crowd into a shade."

Johannes Brahms: Sunday

The great German romantic master Johannes Brahms (1833-1897) spent his life composing every type of piece (except opera), including symphonies, concertos, chamber music, piano music, organ music, and choral music. Like most other composers of the 19th century he composed a great number of songs for voice and piano, and Brahms was certainly a master of the genre. Sunday ("Sonntag") was composed in 1860, and is a simple little tune about a man who hasn't seen his sweetheart all week, and finally sees her going to church on Sunday.

Arthur Sullivan: The Pale Young Curate (from *The Sorcerer*)

W. S. Gilbert (who wrote the words) and Arthur Sullivan (who wrote the music) were one of the most successful theatrical writing teams in history (in terms of fame and commercial success perhaps exceeded only by Rodgers and Hammerstein). Their operettas were full of sharp political satire aimed at the London society of the 1870s, 1880s, and 1890s. *The Sorcerer*, from 1877, is one of their earlier shows, the year before their huge international success with *H.M.S. Pinafore*. The selection featured is a light little comic number in which a minister talks about how ladies of the parish always seem to find a virtuous young pastor particularly attractive. (Pronunciation tip: curate is pronounced "CURE-it).

Giuseppe Verdi: Prayer (from *Simon Boccanegra*)

Giuseppe Verdi (1813-1901) was the most profound and prolific Italian master of opera of the 19th century. He composed 28 operas in his lifetime, even continuing to compose into old age (his last opera was written when he was 80 years old). *Simon Boccanegra*, from 1857, takes place in Genoa of the 14th century. It's a dark tale of political intrigue and corruption. This "Prayer" is a bass aria, sung by a grieving father at the death of his daughter. (Pronunciation: Verdi=VAIR-dee)

Giovanni Bononcini: Arietta (Non posso disperar)

This is a well-known tune from a long-forgotten Baroque Italian opera. It's a song of a dejected lover; the general idea of the words is: "I must not despair, you are so dear to me; my only hope is to endure a sweet pain forever." Cheerful stuff! For nearly the last 100 years it was believed that this piece was by a composer named Severo de Luca, but recent research has revealed the composer as being Giovanni Bononcini (1670-1747). (Pronunciations: Bononcini=bo-known-CHEE-nee; Arietta=ar-ee-EHT-tah)

Scott Joplin: Solace

Scott Joplin (1868-1917) is universally recognized as the most accomplised master of the Ragtime style. Considering this, it's difficult to believe that for most of this century his music languished in obscurity. Joplin's piano pieces were popular during his lifetime, but soon after his death in 1917 his music fell out of the repertory. One can't help but believe that if he had lived just a decade longer, more into the mature recording age, that it would have been a different story. But works of high caliber usually do not go unnoticed forever. The Joplin revival began in the 1970s, and since that time (particularly after the hit movie "The Sting"), his music has been played and loved all over the world. "Solace," written in 1909, is one of Joplin's most elegant rags for piano.

Victor Herbert: Italian Street Song

Victor Herbert (1859-1924) was born in Dublin and grew up in Germany. He had a thorough classical training and became an expert cellist as well as a composer. In 1886 he and his wife were both engaged by the Metropolitan Opera (he as a cellist, she as a singer), and the couple immigrated to New York. While he maintained a "classical" career as a player and conductor, in 1894 he began composing the graceful and carefree operettas that would make him rich and famous. He became the most successful composer that Broadway had seen up until that time. By the time of Herbert's death he had composed over 40 operettas in 30 years, with far more hits than misses. "Italian Street Song" is from *Naughty Marietta* of 1910.

Gaetano Donizetti: Drinking Song (from *Lucrezia Borgia*)

Donizetti (1797-1848) was one of the principal composers of Italian opera in the 19th century. He worked incredibly quickly as a composer, and in about 25 years had written over 50 full-length operas, plus hundreds of other pieces (cantatas, masses, songs, and chamber music). He supposedly could compose an entire opera in less than a week! Donizetti was a highly emotional individual, and there are many anecdotes of his eccentricities. "Drinking Song" is from the opera *Lucrezia Borgia,* composed and premiered in 1833. It's a jolly, fun number, but in the opera the character singing it doesn't realize that his wine has been poisoned, and his merriment is short-lived. Yikes! (Pronunciation: Donizetti=do-nee-TSEHT-tee)

TO MUSIC
(An die Musik)

Franz Schubert

COLLINE'S ARIA
from
LA BOHÈME

Giacomo Puccini

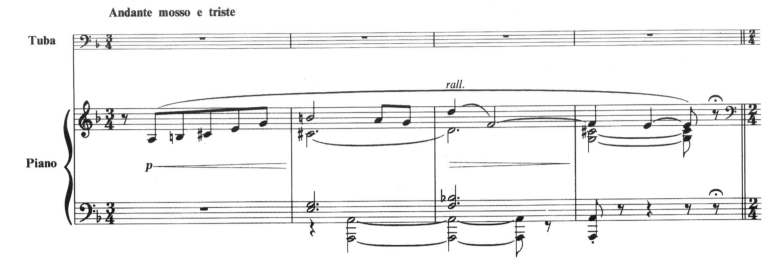

WHO IS SYLVIA?

Franz Schubert

THE SECRET

Gabriel Fauré

WHERE E'ER YOU WALK

George Frideric Handel

double the octave 8va bassa throughout

SUNDAY

Johannes Brahms

THE PALE YOUNG CURATE

from
THE SORCERER

Words by W.S. Gilbert
Music by Arthur Sullivan

Tuba

TO MUSIC
(An die Musik)

Franz Schubert

COLLINE'S ARIA
from
LA BOHÈME

Giacomo Puccini

WHO IS SYLVIA?

Franz Schubert

Moderately

THE SECRET

Gabriel Fauré

Adagio (♪ = 69)

TUBA

WHERE E'ER YOU WALK

George Frideric Handel

SUNDAY

Johannes Brahms

THE PALE YOUNG CURATE

from

THE SORCERER

Words by W.S. Gilbert
Music by Arthur Sullivan

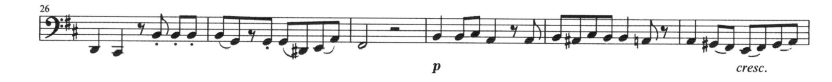

PRAYER
(*Il lascerato spirito*)
from
SIMON BOCCANEGRA

Giuseppe Verdi

Andante sostenuto (♩ = 56)

ARIETTA
(Non posso disperar)

Giovanni Bononcini

SOLACE

Scott Joplin
Arranged by Rick Walters

Repeats are optional repeat

ITALIAN STREET SONG

Victor Herbert

DRINKING SONG
from
LUCREZIA BORGIA

Gaetano Donizetti

PRAYER
(Il lascerato spirito)
from
SIMON BOCCANEGRA

Giuseppe Verdi

ARIETTA
(Non posso disperar)

Giovanni Bononcini

SOLACE

Scott Joplin
Arranged by Rick Walters

Repeats are optional throughout.

ITALIAN STREET SONG

Victor Herbert

Allegro moderato

DRINKING SONG
from
LUCREZIA BORGIA

Gaetano Donizetti

Allegretto ma non troppo

Piano